Nature's Children

PARROTS

Merebeth Switzer

Grolier

FACTS IN BRIEF

Classification of parrots

    Class: *Aves* (birds)

    Order: *Psittaciformes* (parrot-like birds)

    Family: *Psitacidae* (parrots, cockatoos, macaws and lories)

    Genus and Species: There are over three hundred kinds of parrots.

World distribution.   Parrots are found in all the tropical regions of the world.

Habitat.   Tropical forests.

Distinctive physical characteristics.   Usually very brightly colored; feet adapted for climbing and beak that is curved so that the bottom fits into the top.

Habits.   Noisy and long-lived, parrots usually live in large groups. Many are good mimics and can repeat words and other sounds.

Diet.   Mainly fruit and seeds.

Published originally as
"Getting to Know . . . Nature's Children."

This series is approved and recommended by the Federation of Ontario Naturalists.

This library reinforced edition is available exclusively from:

Grolier Educational Corporation
Sherman Turnpike, Danbury, Connecticut 06816

Contents

It is dawn and the jungle is just beginning to stir. Suddenly a loud, raspy screech pierces the air. Another screech, then another. The parrots are awake. They sit on their branches preening and calling, their bright colors glittering through the thick canopy of green leaves. Suddenly they swoop off to look for food. A new day has begun in the tropical forest.

Parrots have been known and loved by people for centuries. Ancient Roman emperors imported them from Africa and the Far East as pets and they have been popular ever since. Why? Most parrot lovers say it is because they are beautifully colored, curious and intelligent, and some can even mimic human speech. Let's take a closer look at these remarkable birds and see what their life is like in the wild.

The brilliantly colored crimson rosella makes its home in Australia.

A Big Family

The parrot family is one of the largest bird families in the world. There are more than 300 different kinds of parrots. The smallest are the tiny pygmy parrots of New Guinea, which are no bigger than the palm of your hand. The largest are the huge, colorful macaws that live in the Amazon. They are as tall as a four-year-old child!

Parrots and parakeets are the most obvious members of the parrot family. But did you know that budgies, cockatoos, cockatiels, lories, lorikeets and lovebirds are also part of the parrot clan?

The peach-faced lovebird is the largest member of its family. Lovebirds get their name from their habit of preening each other.

8

A Place Called Home

Most parrots live high up in the giant trees of the tropical rain forests of the world. However, a few unique parrots that can no longer fly live on the ground. In Australia, some parrots, like cockatoos and budgies, are also found in brush and grassland areas.

Parrots are found mainly on the continents of South America, Africa, Asia and Australia and on the islands in the Pacific Ocean. Some, like the Andean parakeet, can even survive in cool mountain air.

Top: At rest, the sulfur-crested cockatoo keeps its crest close to its head.
Bottom: This is what happens when a cockatoo is alarmed.

A Cracker of a Beak

You can recognize a parrot by its short, chunky, hooked beak. This beak is specially designed for cracking open the nuts and seeds parrots like to eat. The sharp pointed tip of the upper beak also comes in handy for digging into the bark of trees to haul out grubs.

A parrot's powerful beak is useful for more than just finding a meal. Those that live in dense forests sometimes use their beak to grasp branches and vines as they push themselves through the heavy vegetation. Also, a parrot can recover its balance by grabbing a nearby branch with its beak.

Like your fingernails, a parrot's beak is made of hard material that can wear down with use. This is not a problem for the parrot, because the beak keeps growing throughout the bird's life. In fact, if a parrot doesn't eat enough of the hard, crunchy foods that wear down the beak, the bird will have to rub it against a tree trunk or a rock to file it down.

Opposite page:
Macaws exercise their powerful beak by chewing anything within reach.

Family Resemblance

No matter how big a parrot is, its body looks very much like the bodies of all other parrots. Its large, rounded head is joined to its chunky body by a very short neck. The body then tapers from the shoulders, which gives the bird a shape like an upside-down egg.

Because they are mostly strong flyers, parrots have big chest muscles. That is why, when they are sitting, they look like they are wearing a football player's shoulder-pads!

A parrot's feet are very useful for life in the jungle. Why? With two toes facing frontward and two facing backward, the bird can easily climb up and down trees.

Red-crowned parrot.

Fine Feathers . . .

Like all birds, parrots lay eggs and have feathers covering their bodies. There are different kinds of feathers and they serve different purposes.

Very tiny, fluffy, *down* feathers help to insulate the parrot's body, keeping it from getting too cold at night or too hot when the tropical sun beats down during the day. Special *powder down* feathers, which keep growing throughout the bird's life, break off at the tip and crumble into a fine powder. Scientists think this powder helps to keep the parrot from getting soaked and catching a chill during a jungle rainstorm.

The red feathers of this Electus parrot identify it as a female. Males are primarily green.

And Feathers for Flying

Parrots also have *contour* feathers that give their body a streamlined shape for flying. And, of course, their stiff, strong wing feathers give them the ability to fly.

Some parrots—lories and cockatoos, for instance—have short, stubby tails. Others, such as macaws and parakeets, have very long tail feathers. Many of these parrots are extremely powerful fliers. They use their tails for balance and as a rudder to direct them through the air. And some of the long-tailed birds spread out their tail feathers like mini-parachutes to slow them down when they are landing.

The rainbow lorikeet is noisy as it flies from tree to tree, searching for food.

A Rainbow of Colors

Parrots have some of the most beautiful feathers in the animal world. Probably the dullest colored parrot is the African Gray parrot, but even this grayish-white bird has a red rump! The Amazon Green parrots are all different shades of brilliant green, with patches of yellow, red or orange for accent. Some parrots look as though they have had parts of their body dipped in paint. They may be bright pink, electric blue, metallic green or vibrant yellow. Some have all four colors splashed on different parts of their body.

Coat of many colors. (Solitary lory)

Why So Flashy?

In nature, many animals survive by being dull in color to blend in with the world around them. Not the parrot family! In fact, being brilliantly colored helps these birds to survive. How?

Parrots live in jungles where sunlight pokes through the trees and dapples the leaves. The foliage is bright green, and the flowers and fruits are often large and brightly colored. When a parrot sits in a tree in the forest, falcons, hawks and eagles—its most worrisome enemies—may well mistake it for an exotic bloom or a ripe fruit.

The gaudy coloring helps solve another problem parrots sometimes face: finding each other in the dark, thick green jungle. This is especially important if they are looking for a mate. Their brightly colored feathers help. And because both the male and female birds have the same coloring, they can recognize another of their own kind easily.

Opposite page: *Despite its vivid colors, the eastern rosella does blend in with its surroundings.*

Born Mimics

Generally, parrots don't really understand what they are saying, but some of them are great imitators and can copy any sound they hear regularly. This includes the sound of a tomcat howling, a door squeaking or a baby crying. Parrots that have lived with humans since they were very young have sometimes been taught to say many words and even quite long sentences. And because some parrots can live for more than a hundred years in captivity, they have plenty of time to learn new words!

The African Gray parrot is the most skilled mimic of all parrots.

Loud Mouth

While some parrots are noted for their ability to imitate the human voice, others are better known for their very loud, raucous squawks. In fact, people who thought that a parrot would make a good pet have discovered that most of them are noisy and have unpleasant screeching voices. There is a good reason for this. In the jungle, such a loud, unique call helps a parrot to recognize one of its own kind. Also, since a parrot's call can carry for great distances, it helps the birds keep in touch with each other.

The birds with the loudest, most objectionable voices are usually those like the macaws that live in pairs or small groups in the dense jungle. If the closest bird of a parrot's own species is the equivalent of two city blocks away, with a thick screen of vines, trees and flowers in between, a good loud call helps them to find each other.

The blue and yellow macaw is not only loud but is also a good talker.

Sharp Eyes and Ears

With such flashy colors and loud voices it seems obvious that most parrots have keen eyesight and good hearing. This is usually true—in fact, scientists believe that parrots are able to distinguish colors. If parrots saw only in black and white, they would have trouble telling a piece of ripe fruit from leaves or unripe fruit, and they wouldn't be able to identify another of their kind at a distance.

Hearing is also important to parrots, since the thick jungle growth often obscures their view of things. Parrots don't have big, floppy ears. Instead, they have ear openings tucked in under the feathers on the sides of their head. These openings may be small, but they are all a parrot needs to hear perfectly.

Even the eye of the amboina king parrot is beautiful.

On the Menu

Most parrots feed on plants, eating seeds, nuts, fruits, berries, leaves and even fresh green shoots. Seeds and nuts are especially important to some parrots. They use their beak and their big fleshy tongue to get at the food inside.

Have you ever tried to open Brazil nuts without using a nutcracker? Well, just imagine how strong a macaw's beak must be. It can crack open Brazil nuts as easily as you can break a peanut shell.

Scarlet macaw.

A Dinner of Nectar or Worms

The brilliantly colored lories and lorikeets found in New Guinea, Indonesia and Australasia feed on nectar, pollen and fruit. Their beaks are more slender than those of most parrots, and their tongue has a special brush-like tip. They crush the flower blossoms with their beaks and then lap up the drops of nectar.

There are a few parrots that have developed a taste for meat. These birds prefer a dinner of slugs, larvae and wood-boring worms. And cockatoos dig into the ground to find root vegetables similar to potatoes to eat.

The rainbow lorikeet feeds not only on nectar but also on fruit, pollen, berries and insects.

Daily Routine

Most parrots are quite sociable. They spend much of their time together in a flock following the same daily routine. They awaken before sunrise and begin a noisy chorus of calls and screeches. All this noise helps to bond the flock together. It lets each parrot know where the others are, even if it can't see them through the dense vegetation.

After preening their feathers and grooming themselves, the birds move off in search of a good feeding area. There they eat until they are full. Sometimes they may move on to new areas to find more food. Near midday they descend to the cool pools of the forest floor for a drink and a refreshing splash. This is the hottest part of the day, so the parrots pick shady places to rest and relax.

As the cooler evening hours approach, the flock rouses itself and heads off for an evening meal and drink. When darkness sets in, and after a few squabbles over perches, they settle into their treetop roosts and sleep.

Opposite page:
Tidying up!

Finding a Mate

Although many parrots flock together, when nesting time comes most of them pair up to look for a suitable nest. Most parrots mate when they develop their adult feathers at two to four years of age. Some of the larger kinds, however, are not ready to have a family of their own until they are eight to ten years old.

Many types of parrots, including macaws and most Amazon parrots, spend their entire life with one mate. Only if one of the pair dies will the other seek a new mate.

Parrots have different ways of showing their interest in each other. Those that have mated for life roost with their bodies pressed tightly against each other. They also groom each other, and sometimes they kiss and rub each other's necks affectionately.

Birds of a feather stay together.

Parrot Apartments

Almost all parrots nest in holes—in trees, in the ground or among rocks and tree roots. They either take over existing holes, possibly making a few alterations, or they use their strong beaks to hollow out a new hole. Some kinds of parrots even hollow out burrows in termite nests!

Parrot nests don't usually appear to be very comfortable. Unlike many other birds that line their nests with grass and feathers, most parrots lay their eggs right on the scratchy wood chips or whatever else happens to be lying in the hollow they scrape for their eggs.

Like penguins, some parrots nest together in large groups called colonies. For example, the Monk parakeets of South America build their own "apartment buildings." Each pair of birds builds a nest, which they join to other nests with twigs and vines. When the gigantic common nest is completed, each family has its own "apartment."

Macaws nest in holes often well above the ground.

39

Laying Eggs

After the parrots have built their nest, the female begins to lay eggs. Depending on the species, she will lay one to ten pure white eggs, usually one egg every other day. It may take up to two weeks before all her eggs are laid.

Parrots' nests are usually well hidden from the eyes of hungry predators. The eggs are white because they have no need of protective coloring.

The male parrot stays with the female, usually fetching food for her while she sits on the eggs. However, some types of parrots, such as cockatoos, share the egg-sitting duties.

A pair of very rare gang-gang cockatoos.

The Babies Are Born

The eggs hatch about three weeks after they are laid. For some parrots this creates a rather unusual family situation because it means the chicks may be up to two weeks apart in age. With these fast-growing babies, that can make quite a difference!

Newly hatched chicks are not terribly appealing. They are naked, helpless and blind. Fortunately the chicks develop quickly. Within a few days they can see out of their big, bulging eyes and their little bodies are covered in fluffy gray or white down.

The chicks remain in the nest for anywhere from one to three months, and both parents are kept busy feeding them during this time. When the young ones are ready to venture out of the nest, they have a full set of feathers just like their parents and are equipped to fly.

Parrot chicks, like other baby birds, find their first flight tricky. But they are strong and can soon keep up with their parents.

Opposite page: *These Pesquet's parrot chicks will grow up to be large and bulky with a small hawk-like head.*

Growing Up

Even though the young can get around, the parents continue to feed them. For some it may be several more months before they are fully on their own. The parrot chicks use this time to learn about the world around them. Games of chase through the dense jungle help them to master their flying skills. Mock battles to determine who will be the "king of the tree branch" help them learn how to defend their home turf and keep their balance under pressure.

For parrots, growing up is a time to play and a time to become strong so they can survive to raise a family of their own.

Yellow-crowned parrot.

Parrots and People

For generations and in almost all cultures, people have kept parrots as pets. But as their wilderness homes disappear, parrots are becoming rare throughout the world. Most countries now agree that the members of the parrot family, with the exception of a few domestic birds such as budgies, need our protection. It is now illegal in most countries to own or import parrots of any kind for pets. This includes most parrots, macaws and cockatoos. As well, efforts are being made to help preserve the tropical jungles that parrots call home. Many people now realize that these birds are very precious and that it is important to help them survive.

Words to Know

Colony   A large group of parrot pairs nesting in the same area.

Contour feathers   Feathers that help streamline a bird to let it fly through the air more smoothly.

Down   Very soft fluffy feathers.

Flock   A large group of birds.

Hatch   To break out of an egg.

Mate   To come together to produce young. Either member of an animal pair is also the other's mate.

Nectar   The sweet liquid produced by plants.

Plumage   A bird's feathers.

Powder down   Feathers that crumble into fine powder that helps to waterproof the parrot's other feathers.

Preening   Cleaning and oiling the feathers.

INDEX

Cover Photo: Columbus Zoo

Photo Credits: John Cancalosi, pages 4, 15, 16; E.R. Degginger, pages 7, 12, 20; Bill Ivy, pages 8, 35; Cincinnati Zoo, page 11; Zoological Society of San Diego, pages 19, 25, 41; A. Sandrin (Focus Stock Photo), pages 22, 23; Columbus Zoo, pages 27, 31; Kjell Sandved, page 28; Tourism Australia, page 33; Academy of Natural Sciences, pages 36, 39; Ron Garrison (Zoological Society of San Diego), page 43; Y. Arthus-Bertrand (Peter Arnold Inc./Hot Shots), page 45.